Noting Voices:
Contemplating
London's Culture

Haseeb Iqbal

Introduction

This project is about how groundbreaking culture can be born when the rulebook of convention is torn up. It follows a framework of art in which the pre-assigned roles of 'performer' and 'audience member' do not exist. It aims to understand how shaking up such roles can make certain environments and spaces accessible to all, looking at the positive effects this can yield. By contextualising culture, we are able to ground the experiences, and our understanding, of those who offer it; those we are introduced to as icons and geniuses. We begin to see them as humans rather than distant, untouchable forces. This project looks at the power of a two-way exchange in elevating art, where both parties are reliant on each other. It explores a set of spaces and environments that have been underpinned by this ethos, enriching London's cultural landscape in the process. It appreciates the imperative relationship between 'community' and 'space', and shines a light on why we, as a society, depend on these spaces in order to grow.

In school I loved being in all the theatre productions but I was unsettled by how it would be the same group of people auditioning each time. I thoroughly enjoyed the limelight and performative element but what theatre signified to me was a safe space where I could build my confidence and express my voice without restriction, whilst feeling valued and listened to.

The benefits this brought to my life left me baffled as to why this wasn't being encouraged to more people. I saw friends, who I knew would thrive off being given this opportunity, feel totally detached from the idea of ever being a 'theatre person'. They were instead assigned the role of the 'audience person'. Each group were proudly defined by the pre-appointed roles designated for them, both separated distinctly on either side of the fourth wall—with nobody inclined to blur the lines.

Entering the spaces I write about in this book at the age of 15 or 16 was a game-changing point for me. Suddenly these lines were blurred. The performers and audience members could not be distinguished from each other. And there was little to no ownership over embodying a performative role, but rather a collective sentiment that inspired a feeling of participation. I found it empowering. I looked around and saw various strangers being their various selves. I felt I could be whatever version of myself I desired; an identity not defined by either the 'spectator' or 'performer' role that so often seem to dominate creative spaces.

Starting Mare Street Records with some friends was a response to the countless media outlets who appeared to be jumping on the hype-train of a community that was clearly generating some attention amongst youngsters. They tended to quantify this cultural shift as 'the London Jazz Scene'—perhaps the most frequently assigned term used to describe this community. I aimed to take it back to the foundations of the scene by starting a podcast platform through which I could relaxedly converse with figureheads and personalities who I deeply respect. Whose observations and insights could help illuminate the magic of what was going on with a depth and intimacy that was yet to be seen through the endless articles and spreads that seemed to be coming from all corners of the globe. Whilst all of the journalism centered on the culture, few outlets seemed to take it back to the source—the space—and those who facilitated it. This project focuses primarily on five of the seven conversations I have had so far, tuning into five personalities who have been vital backbones, and mouthpieces, in serving one of the most fascinating cultural shifts the capital has seen for a while. It aims to take the quality of conversation I enjoyed one step further, converting it into a medium that is both tangible and physical. It aims to cross-reference the conversations, illuminating a sense of polyvocality across various topics that are discussed with each guest in hope of adding some context to the culture.

Point of reference for who I have conversed with and their roles within the story:

Episodes of Mare Street Records which this project primarily focuses on

Episode 2: Marina Blake
—Founder and Creative Director of Brainchild Festival:
Created in 2012 by a 19 year old Marina and a bunch of fellow first-year university students, born from a pureness of ignorance and ambition, Brainchild's DIY-run, volunteer-led, small-scale ethos has always been a commitment to ensure that it's 'a place to manifest ideas'. For the last eight years it has championed the bold ideas of young people, offering a platform for many to experiment, having aided and nurtured some of the city's most exciting creatives in the process. Its uniquely sponsor-free, community-driven approach has kept it limited to under 3000 people, allowing togetherness and collaboration to thrive, whilst redefining the perception of what a festival embodies.

Episode 3: Alexis 'Lex' Blondel
—Founder of Total Refreshment Centre (TRC):
Also formed in 2012 within an inconspicuous Edwardian warehouse space behind a petrol station in Stoke Newington, north London, Lex and some friends acquired this building through an unappealing Gumtree advert. It had historically served as a chocolate factory, gearbox factory and radiant Caribbean social club. Repurposing it into a recording studio, workshop and live music event space, TRC soon became the nucleus for a beaming community to congregate and create within. It also became a pivotal space for performing musicians to take risks, allowing London's jazz heads to both collaborate and grow in organic, refreshing ways, as well as connecting live music and DJ culture in a raw form that had not been seen before.

Hackney Council's revoking of their licence in 2018 saw their stint as a venue sadly come to an end, however they have continued to thrive as a studio, record label and ever-growing community.

Episode 4: Wayne Francis aka Ahnansé
—Founder of Steam Down:
Born in the summer of 2017 as a weekly Wednesday jam night at a bar in Deptford, south east London, Steam Down came as a product of Wayne's busy touring routine that had put him out of touch with jamming alongside other musicians on a regular basis. He formed it for the purpose of connecting instrumentalists and vocalists, and has built it since as a community who have radically shifted the face of London jazz. An environment that offers hypnotic poetry alongside thumping bass rhythms on the same evening, Steam Down has allowed many of London's younger musicians a platform to grow under the guidance of Wayne. Additionally, it has had the likes of more established musicians such as Kamasi Washington, Shabaka Hutchings, Nubya Garcia and more all pass through on multiple occasions. As well as forming into a collective, Steam Down has been a driving force for taking the sound of this scene forwards into uncharted territories.

Episode 6: Slam the Poet
—former Creative Director of STEEZ:
An absolutely pivotal pillar, the STEEZ community manifested itself in 2012 in the form of monthly meet-ups, most often on the last Sunday of each month, taking over a pub somewhere in south east London. It would be an organic template, combining an open jam session, an open mic, various live bands and performing poets alongside a receptive, warm, excited crowd in the form of their friends. At points, it would bring club levels of energy into the pub—an informal platform and safe space for many of London's jazz musicians and performers to experiment with and develop their craft. It allowed them to collaborate with each other on

different projects and find their identity through less pressured performances; an instrumental cornerstone to the story that had its focus on the fun.

Episode 7: Errol Anderson
—Founder of Touching Bass:
Founded towards the end of 2014 by Errol, initially as a mix series for VICE's 'Noisey' when he was a full-time journalist, Touching Bass are a movement, community and curational platform sustained by a wide group of people, rooted in the ethos of music bringing people together. Formed of various different musical windows, Touching Bass are best known for their seminal club nights, of which the primary focus is placed on dancing. As well as that, they host various live music events, communal discussions and listening sessions—a range of lenses encapsulated through their NTS Radio show which sheds light on it all. They have recently developed into a label and continue to push forward London's musical landscape in bold, innovative ways.

Each of these people are united in one thing: they have facilitated the space for culture to be birthed and developed. Through that, they have maintained communities who have all had the ability to tune into something greater than themselves. They have done so unconventionally, rewriting the rulebook in the process and subsequently have advanced a moment into a movement.
A movement centred around a core, nucleus community and widened over time. I must raise, however, that although these five entities are key pillars in the sustenance of London's musical renaissance, I am yet to converse with those behind Jazz Re:Freshed and Tomorrow's Warriors; the other two foundations that are of equal importance within this story, in my opinion. Perhaps a part two beckons. What I set out to write is by no means an objective analysis of what this community represents, nor a full-length timeline, but rather a project that responds to the listed

conversations, using those as a framework to delve deeper into a handful of the topics touched on, trying to make sense of a scene so rich, pure, and, in this day and age, powerfully unique.

When we look at Brainchild Festival, Total Refreshment Centre, STEEZ, Steam Down and Touching Bass, we are faced with a spectacle whereby all sense of hierarchy is eliminated. It is this dismantling of hierarchy in creative spaces that, in my opinion, is the central reason as to how and why this scene has flourished with such authenticity. And why it will continue to flourish for a long while. It is this central philosophy which has helped spawn several strands of magic; an unconventional template that has yielded unprecedented levels of quality, forged through the premise of community.

Despite being tight-knit communities in each of their own rights, having entered each as an outsider I was struck by the lack of tribalism that seemed to dominate these environments. It is the approachability of these spaces that lend them an air of attainability to those who may feel overwhelmed or unwelcomed when wandering into a community that is to any extent established by a set of core people. The conventional assumption is that anything prescribed by the term 'scene' might be too cool or contained. Why enter a different community when I can remain in my community? Around people I know well and feel myself around. These notions have appeared widespread amongst friends who have been reluctant to come and see what all the fuss is about and to an extent I can understand that strand of thinking. My observation on this musical community is that it is satisfied with its identity yet ever-expanding through the new people that join it and the energies and ideas that join them. These aren't spaces that will drag you into them but spaces that will welcome you in and look out for you if you treat them with the respect and attentiveness expected. It is whole-heartedly built off an exchange and it soon becomes clear when present that all parties have to do their bit in order for the magic to blossom.

Eliminating hierarchy

Through subverting the conventions of what a space that serves entertainment entails, these communities have broken down barriers, making them accessible and accommodating to more people. Speaking to Marina Blake of Brainchild Festival in Episode 2 of Mare Street Records, it became clear to me the importance of setting up the festival at the naïve and excited age of just 19 in anchoring the ethos that has been set ever since. "At that age there's a lot of talk and a lot of ideas. This was meant to show that with enough hard work and enough people coming together, amazing things that you never thought could happen, could happen."

"Doing it at 19 was a really important benchmark as it was meant to show people that they could take their new ideas—and the things they had just started to study at university about the world—seriously and have a voice within that."

The relationship between 'ideas' and 'a voice' is crucial. Many ideas are lost through feeling inferior to, or removed from, the identity of 'a creative'. Young people who aren't offered a platform to bolster their confidence, or voice their thoughts, will often settle for consuming ideas rather than performing them, before that pre-designated role becomes acutely entrenched in their mind. Brainchild flip these conventions on their head; a festival with no VIP or backstage area; where all performers and ticket-holders camp together, primarily volunteer-run and totally sponsor-free with security guards as relaxed as the punters; a festival which you can walk the entire circumference of in just a few minutes.

Arriving at my first Brainchild in 2016 with two mates as a set of underage 16 and 17-year-olds with fake IDs, a youthful curiosity and an awareness of certainly being the youngest there, I was immediately taken back by the human element of an experience that I thought was meant to separate me from those who were providing the vibes.

Feeling star-struck by a scintillating headliner on the main stage on the Friday evening was a relatively comfortable feeling. Waking up sweaty and sticky the next morning, arched delicately over a fickle tap whilst attempting to cleanse myself in 30 seconds and seeing the same headliner stood beside me confronted with the same primitive task was a rather unfamiliar sensation. However, it was one of deep comfort. A reassuringly humanising moment that strangely aligned me with the magic I had witnessed the evening before. Suddenly talent through the lens of performance didn't overpower me with any sense of superiority or 'superstar' complex. It felt strangely within reach.

In our conversation, Marina outlines three principal elements that she says underpins Brainchild:

Community—We have been aiming to build an organic community of people that have been trying to support each other and listen to each other to the next level; whether it's art, politics or on a social scale.

Bold ideas—To challenge the status quo and provide an antidote to the general crapness.

Celebrating DIY spirit—The idea of 'we know you haven't really done this before but here's a platform for you to try it out.'

The Sunday morning of 2016's edition saw an open mic hosted by Slam the Poet at the STEEZ Café; a stage that was run by the STEEZ crew with a focus on jam sessions and more relaxed performances for smaller artists, formed within a rectangular marquee space with a small stage at the front, a bar at the back and often an array of seated folk in between. As always with the STEEZ open mics, I was warmed by the supportive, engaged set of listeners and I summoned the confidence to jump up and perform a poem in front of a crowd of total strangers. I remember Slam encouraging the audience to cheer for me and my colourful shorts, a gesture that very much put me at ease before delivering my piece. The response was sincere—I felt listened to and appreciated—and I sat back down with a warmth that lifted me and helped me realise that this place was clearly different to any other I'd encountered.

Applying to perform for the following year's edition in the months that followed was more an excuse to not revise for my A Levels for an evening rather than actually believing I would be successful. However, at that point, I was not aware of the third bullet point Marina outlined in our more recent chat and before I knew it, I was given the opportunity to perform at The Forum stage on the Saturday evening of Brainchild's 2017 edition.

Approachability

I have seen a parallel between the approachability of a space and the instinctual, unstructured nature of the person who is behind it. These spaces have all emanated from a place of genuineness,

Brainchild Festival – 15/7/18 – Sons of Kemet headline the mainstage, accompanied by the crescent moon and a shimmering Mars. Photo credit: Jordan Matyka

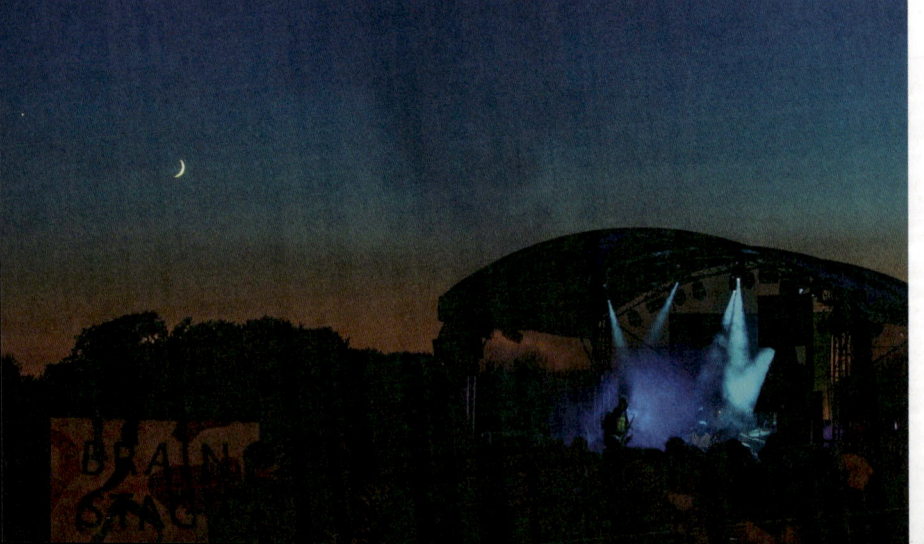

aided by a bold vision and a team of people who believe in this vision, willing to work hard to maintain it.

Lex's impulsive desire is what made him follow up a terrible Gumtree advert for a seemingly dilapidated, obsolete space behind a petrol station in north London. This approach, combined with repurposing it alongside a team of individuals, to serve different functions, with the main aim of bringing people together, is not only the mindset that birthed Total Refreshment Centre but it is the mindset that has continued to uphold it.

Speaking to me in Episode 3, a few months after TRC lost its licence as a venue, reflecting on what was most precious to him, Lex expressed, "The beauty of it was people being able to come to me and say 'I've got this idea, I want to do something' and then that becoming an exchange and building something together, rather than looking at them as just a booking."

Lex's choice of words, 'just a booking', highlights how the artistry of musicians is often diluted by venues and promoters into an economic asset, agreed from a place of certainty where there is less risk but inevitably less reward.

The power of 'building something together' cannot be underestimated when it comes to nurturing incredible culture on a grassroots level. If there is an element of enthusiasm between both parties, not only is the end-product bound to be special but the process of getting there will be too.

Marina has exemplified this idea of togetherness and risk-taking through how she runs Brainchild when deciding to get four-piece group, Asoma, to headline the Saturday night of 2018's festival despite having never heard anything from them and them having never released any music. Formed of Maxwell Owin, Jack Stephenson-Oliver, Jake Long and Ben Hayes, all of whom had played the festival several times across various different projects, Marina emphasised in our chat, "It's born out of the relationship element." Her instinct drove the decision and the performance was brilliant. There is real merit in lacking structure and certainty, something that is compounded through Lex's words, "If something excites me and even if nobody knows you, I'll say let's give it a go."

Conducting my conversations with both Lex and Marina, I wondered how far this 'championing the unchampioned' ethos could go. I pondered the role of sentimentality in perhaps blurring this outlook when acts, who had built relationships with them over time, got bigger and started to require higher fees, handled with more of a professional set-up. Would that be able to co-exist with their DIY structure? For Lex, this idea was quite clear-cut: "It's most exciting to work at the early stages of things, for me. When booking agents and labels come into the equation, I am stoked for the artists but I know I have done my part." He acknowledges his role as the grassroots cultivator and finds great pleasure in helping smaller acts find their potential, straying away from the commercial inclinations that have inevitably been put to him in the past.

However, running a venue year-round is very different to curating a festival which exists for just three days a year. Especially one that has been built around a loyal community of musicians who would play annually on a low-budget scale. To offer a glimpse into the indispensable role Brainchild Festival has played for this 'scene', every single musician that was part of Brownswood's 2018 *We Out Here* compilation, curated by Gilles Peterson, that aimed to illuminate 'London's jazz scene', has played at the festival; whilst most have performed several times over since its earliest edition. For Marina, the popular boom that seemed to encircle these musicians in the months after Brainchild's 2017 edition was a daunting reality that meant many of the regulars were now too expensive to book.

"My only advice to anyone is that time is really great, you learn a lot. The repositioning of people that I would normally book, realising that they are now headliners, I thought 'where does that leave us?' If Brainchild is a platform for emerging people then we must reconsider our position. My biggest advice to myself looking back at it is just trust that if you book with the same values and the same principles, built on forming relationships, it will work out," she told me. The words 'same values and same principles' ring loudest, whilst her description of it as a festival 'built on forming relationships' aligns with Lex's notion of connecting with people and 'building something together'. The longevity of these communities isn't just established through the long-term relationships they have formed over the years but through their openness to keep connecting to new energies, underpinned by a constant curiosity for what's fresh.

Instinct

My observations have led me to believe that all great visionaries trust their own instinct before anybody else does. Something that is only recognised in the long-term when, in this case, the same artists and collectives that they provided a platform to before anybody else wanted to are now acknowledged as a mainstream facet. Eight-piece Afrobeat collective KOKOROKO performing a 90-minute set at this year's BBC Proms, Steam Down collective performing on *Later... with Jools Holland,* The Comet is Coming and Ezra Collective playing on Glastonbury's West Holts stage, Sons of Kemet headlining Somerset House. These events didn't mysteriously occur but it's easy to forget about the source and the story of the culture that we consume when accessing it on such a mainstream level. If it wasn't for these grassroots entities and the risk-taking, impulse-driven personalities that propelled them then none of this radiant culture would exist for mass audiences.

Perhaps a dialogue between mainstream, more established bodies of culture and the grassroots spaces and communities, that helped cultivate what they now platform further down the chain, could be a positive mechanism to increase awareness of where the culture comes from. If these foundational, DIY-run communities are constantly lacking the sustainability and protection they deserve, yet are aiding mainstream culture a few years later, then surely it is in the best interest of all to ensure we safeguard the spaces and communities who are at a constant threat of ever-rising rent and incongruous council decisions.

Gentrification; solutions over sentiments

The topic of gentrification is a complex one that could have taken up this entire book. It is a sad reality that acts as a looming cloud, hovering above the communities whose nuclei are defined by its existence. However, it is also something that undeniably aids this city's cultural landscape in certain instances, making the commonplace 'fuck gentrification' sentiment neither feasible nor productive. As Wayne Francis of Steam Down points out in Episode 4, gentrification is an inevitable reality that exists within the capitalist framework. "London is the heart of capitalism," he says. "It's where money is made and everything is based around that. If someone comes to the landlord and says 'I'm going to give you more money', they will say 'yeah'."

Speaking about why there is such an issue with acquiring space in the capital Wayne tells me, "A lot of the people who own stuff in the city don't live here, so they are not immersed in the culture. And if you're not immersed, it doesn't really mean much to you." Wayne's ability to acknowledge the other side's perspective is a vital first step, illuminating the importance of a reciprocal dialogue when discussing this issue.

It occurs to me that there's an understandably emotion-fuelled anti-gentrification sentiment amongst the young. However, it predisposes many to voice, agree and echo their disenchantment with the system, without offering much of a solution as to how to tackle it.

A lot of us play an undeniable role of complicity in an issue we are deeply critical of. Until we are able to see that, acknowledge our role and speak about pragmatic solutions, very little will change.

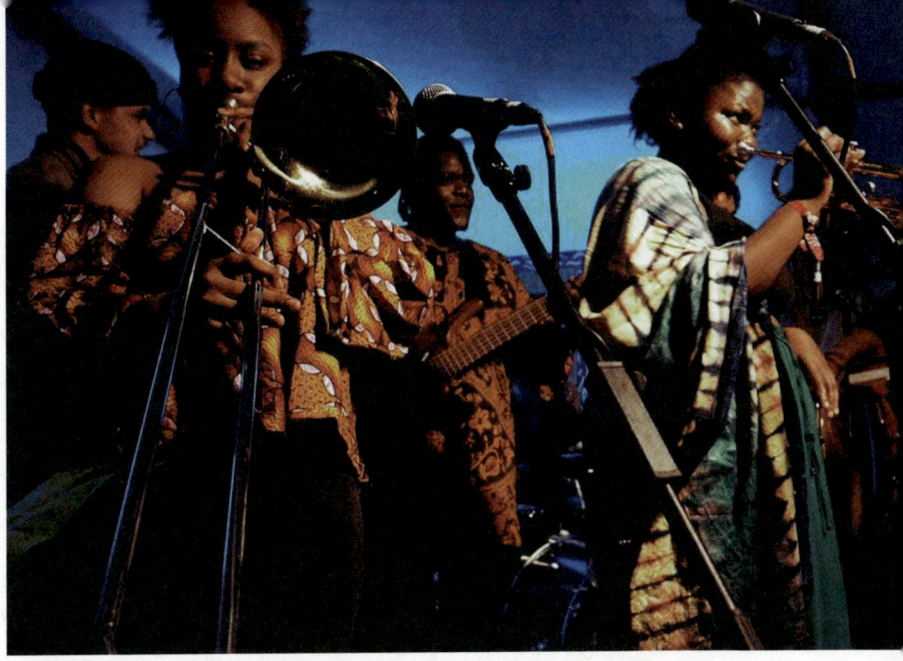

Brainchild Festival – 9/7/16 – KOKOROKO perform at the STEEZ Café stage, following on from Ezra Collective and Puma Blue.

  I've seen enough friends posting anti-gentrification Guardian articles on their social media, expressing their disapproval, being validated by their friends, before drinking at £6 pint establishments that same evening with those same very people. Social media dilutes any sense of proactiveness, distilling it down to self-affirmation in the form of comments and likes, to self-willingly deceive the subject, making them feel that they've done their bit.

  In order to make progress in navigating this destructive issue that is unapologetically displacing many communities, we must engage with the decision-makers who are in charge. That requires building bridges of communication with them rather than shutting them down and vilifying them for what they do. At the end of the day, what they do makes sense to them but it doesn't make sense to us. What we believe makes sense to us but it doesn't resonate with them. Therefore, there is a communication gap that, if we want things to change, we must bridge.

Errol Anderson of Touching Bass, who grew up in Bow, east London, says in Episode 7 that he is understanding of why people move into new areas, since "they just want cheaper housing for themselves." However, the trait that agitates him most is how "there is such a lack of acknowledgement of the space that they're moving into," adding that "it doesn't take much effort to acknowledge and understand the cultures that have been there before you." Errol references somebody who started a yoga retreat that recently cropped up next to a Nigerian church in Peckham, south east London, before complaining that the noise from the church was disturbing the yoga classes. There is a clear conflict of interests that appears to be quite contradictory amongst people who move into areas with a historically layered cultural fabric. The idea of wanting to be living in a vibrant quadrant of the capital that is booming and bustling appears appealing and 'cool'. Yet the feeling of entitlement that can drive the experience of newcomers, highlighted through their dismissiveness of local communities is the most problematic factor. It must begin with our acknowledgement of what role we are playing in the issue and which communities have helped form the fabric of the area that we now live in, before working out how we can engage with that.

How can we do our bit? Get our food from the independent grocery shops or markets. Eat out and support independent, local restaurants. Speak to the people who serve us and make an effort to try and connect with them. Research the history of the area we are moving into and handle ourselves with an awareness of this. Recognising that we are part of the issue isn't useless and shouldn't be a defeatist fact; it is the first step to inspiring a change in how we act.

I ask Errol what new music venues can do to further integrate with the areas they arrive into, as well as welcome the local communities who have pre-existed such spaces. Wayne Francis's Steam Down was allowed to begin on a Wednesday evening as a weekly jam at newly-opened bar Buster Mantis in

Deptford as a free-entry occurrence which opened it up to many different demographics, since affordability wasn't an issue. This certainly complimented the buzz which propelled the night forward at an unprecedented pace, however, I mention to Errol an anecdote of an experience I had at a Caribbean restaurant on Deptford High Street during the early days of Steam Down.

I got speaking to a Jamaican man in his 60s at this local food joint and he started asking me about if anything exciting happens "around here anymore." The word 'anymore' a precursor to the nostalgia he went on to speak with, recalling the reggae parties of the 70s and 80s with such fondness, however referring to the exciting cultural happenings of south east London as a thing of the past as far as he was concerned. In the days before Steam Down had garnered much of a hype, I passionately spoke to him about this "crazy weekly jazz night which had the most immense energy, sweat and vibes." He was intrigued and asked me where this was. I described to him where Buster Mantis was. "Oh. That trendy looking cocktail bar down the road?" He hesitated as I nodded my head, tucking into my exquisite jerk chicken, rice and peas. "I don't feel welcome there," he continued. I went on to explain to him that he shouldn't feel that way as it's such a welcoming event and at the start of every jam Wayne Francis asks all newcomers to put their hands up and gets everybody to welcome them in with a warm round of applause. I told him it's multi-generational and everyone who comes cannot stop coming. "Oh, and also. It's free too!" He couldn't believe what I was saying and became occupied with a sense of deep excitement. "I'm going to be there next week, man. Thank you so much. I had no idea," he told me.

It was a warm and refreshing interaction, however, it left me slightly unsettled. I mention to Errol in our chat that it was sad that I had to be the person to tell this local who has lived in Deptford for most of his life that he should feel welcome at a local bar down his road. It probed me to wonder if a venue like Buster

Mantis, which markets itself online as an 'independent, family-run, Jamaican establishment', could do more to accommodate the locals who are part of the identity they suggest they are part of too. The owner may have Jamaican roots and the bar's name may resemble a post-colonial leader of Jamaica, however its £8 cocktails and primarily newly-moved young professional clientele clearly doesn't familiarise or welcome many of the local Caribbean population. It wasn't that this man didn't want to come into Buster Mantis. It's that he didn't feel like he could approach it or relate to it. And venues who are entering such areas, as evident products of gentrification, must be expected to actively engage with the local communities who live there.

As somebody who loves music, I can often become deceived that if I feel welcomed and excited by a space I am in, then it is a positive force for all. However, meeting the man in the restaurant that evening illuminated the importance of looking out for, and remembering, local communities in areas. The moment they feel disillusioned with the new spaces around them, irrespective of the space's intention, something has gone wrong and that needs to be rectified. Errol agrees with me that a place like Buster Mantis "can definitely do more."

Having said this, I do believe Buster Mantis providing a free and exciting weekly music night which harboured an inclusive atmosphere is an admirable first step, as well as a useful template for other newly-opened venues and bars to observe. However, I don't believe that it's enough.

I think it's important that we, the consumers of culture in this city, who uphold and sustain these new spaces, put pressure on such venues and bars to ensure they do more to integrate with the local communities from the area. Whether it's offering a space for people at local schools, colleges or youth clubs to perform at. Or collaborating with local charities that are invited to host events there. At the end of the day a new bar is a new space. And space can go a long way if used with the right intentions, especially in a city where accommodative space feels all too rare.

We have an ability to be able to make an impact, and a duty to do so, amidst the destructive pace of something as unforgiving as gentrification. It's something everybody's required to be hyper-aware of, as well as responsive towards. These suggestions certainly aren't a total solution to an issue so deep-rooted and detrimental, however, they are an achievable first step that we can all be part of.

There's no community without space

This project explores a range of communities. Yet the alignment between both community and physical space is inextricable, hence why each of these communities have been defined, and formed, through having access to space.

To understand this current movement of music in London which he is helping spearhead, Wayne Francis opts to look at the capital's music scene 15 years prior to what we're seeing now, when he was growing up, highlighting the importance of space being affordable in order for great culture to be born.

"If we look at the broken beat era of music," mentioning the likes of Kaidi Tatham, Dego 2000 and Mark de Clive-Lowe. "That whole group of people created music that wasn't heard at that time; it was completely new and completely London-based. If you saw them live, you'd see everything from the beats and the DJs to the live bands, everything!" The importance of being able to visually view all elements of music in the live setting is a crucial part of a musician's self-growth. Wayne's observations of seeing how live music and electronic music aligned in the flesh, at the broken beat nights, evidently informed his own musical path. This was seen a few years later when he formed the collective Myriad Forest, which combined the live vibrations of Yussef Dayes on drums, Jamie Benzies on bass guitar and the late David Turay on saxophone, whilst accompanied by the electronics of Tilé Gichigi-Lipere aka D'Vo, forming a musical arc that somewhat echoed what the broken beat guys were doing.

Speaking about his experience of those broken beat nights, Wayne continues, "That was all in west London when it was affordable. And now there are hardly any venues in west London, maybe one or two." The rise in property prices in west London inevitably pushed these musicians away from the area, however the issue is more convoluted than just them having to relocate. Wayne tells me how he found it hard to connect with these older musicians since they had left the area and the community was no longer revolved around the local spaces it previously had been.

"The problem with communities changing so fast is that you lose out on mentorship." A compounding point which emphasises the pivotal role physical spaces play in nurturing communities. The faster property prices rise without any sense of council regulation or recognition, communities

STEEZ – 4/4/15 – Sheila Maurice-Gray, Shirley Tetteh and Nubya Garcia at The Fox and Firkin, Lewisham. Photo credit: Matthew Kirby

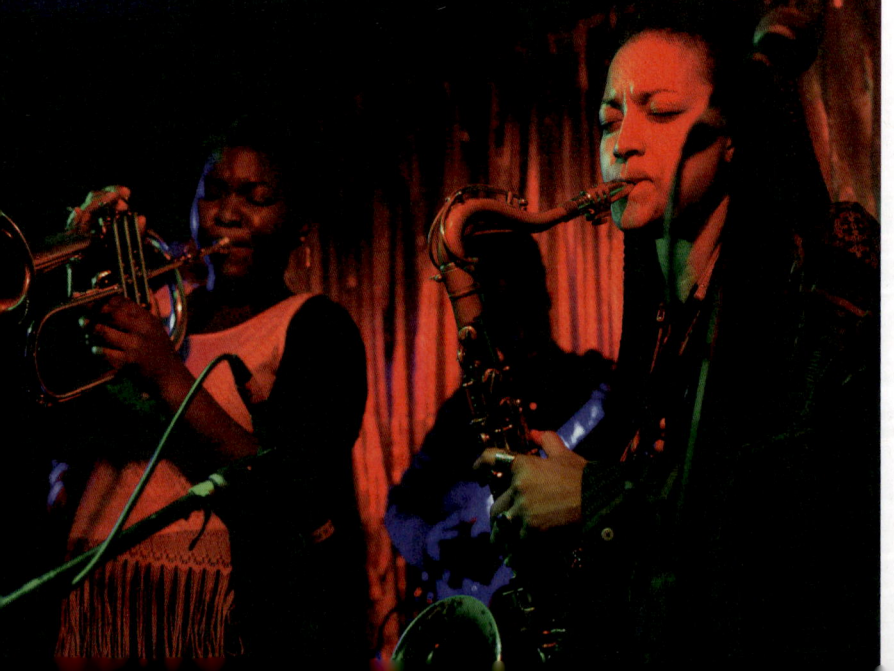

will continue to be ripped apart and the culture that is aided through such spaces will struggle to grow and exist.

Mentorship, institutional structures and the purpose they offer

Wayne mentions how the precarious nature of space in London makes him extra appreciative and in awe of something like Tomorrow's Warriors; an educational jazz organisation with a focus on artist development and mentorship across underrepresented backgrounds. It was founded in 1991 by Janine Irons MBE and Gary Crosby OBE, based at the Southbank Centre and, most crucially, has provided all of its mentorship services for free. Its fundamental role, spread over a long period of time, is accentuated through Wayne being able to recall esteemed musicians both older than him, citing the likes of Soweto Kinch and Shabaka Hutchings, as well as younger than him, namely Nubya Garcia, Sheila Maurice-Gray, Moses Boyd and Femi Koleoso, who have all been served fundamentally by the organisation.

"That's why this scene is so healthy. Because it is rooted in something that allows knowledge to be passed down." A statement buttressed by how many of the, now, more established musicians, including Wayne, have continued to return to help mentor those younger than him. It is a scene that has always thrived off an exchange. And it is this personal, cross-generational exchange that is so valuable.

The importance of it being free is something that Shabaka Hutchings has referred to as vital since it means that "economic mobility is no longer a factor for children deciding to take up music." He adds, in a video raising awareness about financially protecting the institution, "If you care about jazz music and care about how it looks not just now, but how it's going to look in the future, for me, this is an investment in the face of the British land." Whilst Ezra Collective's Femi

Koleoso refers to it as "a champion for keeping jazz alive and keeping it equal."

The role of equality is key since Tomorrow's Warriors has been an absolutely imperative enterprise for diversifying the musical landscape of UK Jazz; a foundational pillar within this story. The Coronavirus outbreak has this year led them to start a crowd-funding scheme under the title #IAMWARRIOR2020. They seek to raise £100,000 after having lost 112 live gigs between March and September this year, wiping away 100% of their income stream required to support their free workshops which, for 30 years, have been facilitating space and mentorship for over 10,000 aspiring musicians aged between 11-25; primarily focusing on Black talent and young women; the most historically under-represented demographics in this country's jazz scene. The risk of one of the most historically stable, egalitarian structures within this London jazz story having to potentially charge for lessons for the first time since its inception jeopardises not having, what co-founder Janine Irons MBE refers to as, "a music industry which reflects the diversity of the society in which we live." She believes that charging would result in participants being "mostly white middle-class and mostly boys;" a set of demographics whose historic over-representation has been crucially subverted by Tomorrow's Warriors in recent years.

Reversing this progress would be damaging to the diversity of this country and the cultural landscape that drives it. If diversity in art is something we value, then programmes such as Tomorrow's Warriors must be subsidised and supported by those at the top. As well as yielding a depth of talent for this country's music scene, it offers children from less privileged backgrounds a point of focus and purpose; something especially crucial at this time. The YMCA revealed in their January 2020 report that every region of England has seen funding for youth services cut by more than 60% since 2010, with areas in the North and Midlands seeing up to 80% of services slashed. It is perhaps no coincidence that a rise in youth violence and gang-related activity has directly correlated with this statistic; young people need something to identify with and a purpose that offers them a voice as well as a sense of value. If youth services, sports or music programmes aren't on offer, they will find their identity through other ways. Meanwhile those in positions of privilege will have no issue getting the resources they can more-easily afford, dangerously widening a social gap that this diverse music scene has helped bridge in recent years.

The role of informal spaces

Whilst Wayne recognises the unequivocal importance of something like Tomorrow's Warriors, which passes on that experience of mentorship, he acknowledges however that it is an institution which embodies an element of formality. He speaks of the merit in music being able to flow organically from one musician to another in a more laid-back environment. This idea chimes with what Marina Blake mentions to me in our conversation when speaking about the instrumental role of something less institutional like STEEZ. As a monthly night in a south east London pub where friends would get together whilst at school or university, it was a pillar that thrived off its informality, coexisting in complementary form alongside more institutional structures such as Tomorrow's Warriors and Trinity Laban, where many of the musicians were studying.

"It was a space where they could get together which was not institutional. They could jam, play new stuff, it would get sweaty a bit like a club. Everyone there was their age or younger and thought it was brilliant," she tells me. "It was the first time these musicians saw all their friends, and those friends' friends digging this stuff." STEEZ offered an avenue of experimentation for these musicians who, at the same time, were all learning the formal structures of jazz music at their respective institutions. It offered a balance to their craft, allowing them to find their own voices in less pressured, less educational environments.

It was underpinned by unprecedented levels of energy, which sometimes saw over 700 people attending it at the Fox and Firkin pub in Lewisham, as well as a very engaged, warm and receptive crowd who felt as much a part of STEEZ as those who orchestrated and performed at it. Once again, it was the relaxed nature of the pub setting that dismantled the hierarchy within the space, allowing cypher sessions, poetry readings, live jams and performing bands to all be received in a democratic manner that involved all people present; a sense of egalitarianism rare within the creative arts.

The importance of casual space in aiding enthralling culture is something that is as recognised by the performing musicians as it is by those who receive it. Saxophonist Binker Golding, of Binker and Moses, when speaking to Dazed Magazine following the closure of Total Refreshment Centre in the summer of 2018 spoke of its qualities, reflecting on having played there and having recorded the album *Alive in the East?* in its studio.

"TRC ended up playing such a pivotal role because it was a venue that was never afraid to give musicians time and space in order for them to develop their craft on-stage. This is extremely rare. Most venues want the finished product, not an experiment. They want to book an established act doing something they know will work and will sell, not a bunch of youngsters they've never heard of who are taking risks in front of a paying audience. In doing so, they helped develop a culture and scene that's now internationally recognised. In every European country we tour, people ask us about this scene and they bring up TRC like they're talking about your wife." Speaking of how most venues are not willing to book 'an experiment', Binker illustrates the importance of not only consuming culture in a non-hierarchical environment, but the importance of building one's artistry in such environments. This is epitomised by his conclusion of TRC as a space.

"It's the venue that put on a whole load of unknown acts at a time when much bigger, better known venues didn't have the

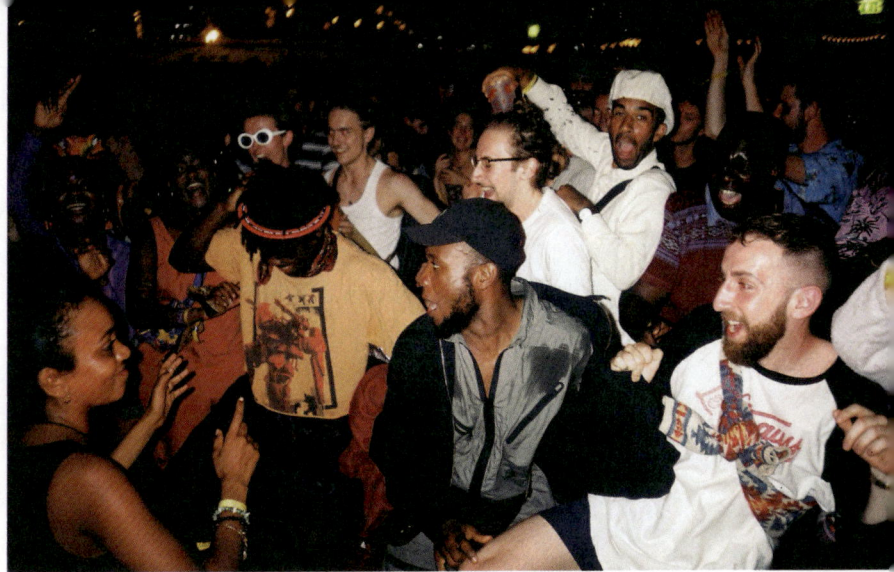

STEEZ Café stage at Brainchild Festival – 8/7/17 – Me, centre right, a few hours after my poetry performance. Photo credit: Slam the Poet

guts to do so. They took the chance and in doing so became a vital part of this movement. Now other venues, up and down the country, are falling over themselves trying to get a piece of what TRC essentially nurtured, when initially a lot of these places wouldn't have touched some of these bands with a barge pole."

Social media presence; a requirement or a desire?

Marina Blake makes a link between pivotal grassroots bodies of culture from the past and more mainstream cultural lenses of now. Referring to STEEZ, she speaks of the "record sales that are now happening across the likes of Brownswood" and other labels. She says that the "target audiences" of these labels "were very much developed at STEEZ;" a fact that many forget when accessing this music through more established channels and outlets.

It is the instrumental role STEEZ has played for a bustling movement that unsettles Marina when speaking about STEEZ's decision to remove its historical digital footprint, deleting its Facebook, Instagram and website after its abrupt ending as an event towards the end of 2017. She mentions that it is writing itself out of history through evading any online presence, maintaining that it's not necessarily a bad thing since its significance will always exist. However, she concludes that, "if people are so fixated with the story (of this scene) then we must acknowledge its role," and having no social media or online footprint makes this very difficult.

Speaking to one of the directors and key personalities who helped run STEEZ, Slam the Poet, in Episode 6 of Mare Street Records, I raise Marina's point about its lack of media presence impeding its legacy from being recognised and celebrated. I compare this to Lex's Total Refreshment Centre who, after the loss of the venue, continued to build as a community, collaborating with the likes of Blue Note and spaces such as the Barbican and Dimensions Festival, using its social media to continue to communicate with its community despite not having a physical nucleus to congregate within. I question the value of immortalising a thing of the past through a social media presence.

Slam tells me that professionally it has had its negative impacts: "How can I prove to a venue that we brought 700 people to a pub" when intending to throw an event now. "But in a way that was also the point and I do still stand by that." They mention

Total Refreshment Centre – 15/5/15 – Yussef Kamaal perform first ever gig.
Photo credit: Alexis Blondel

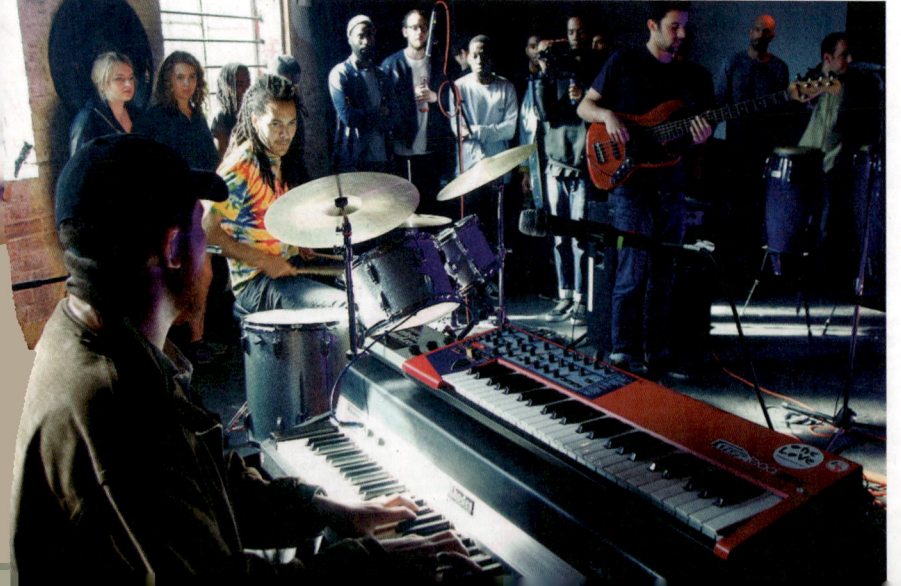

that from the beginning of helping run the event, the philosophy was 'you have to be here to understand it'; a notion that all who helped run it deeply agreed with.

Slam makes a fascinating point about the value of refraining from creating a social media account of what STEEZ did, relating it to the idea of storytelling. "A storyteller is forced to choose certain details. You can never tell everything that happens in the room."

"For STEEZ to be an open platform that anybody could enter into, it had to not claim a narrative. It had to instead make possible several narratives at once," Slam says, referring to the ethos that it harboured at its nights.

STEEZ's magic is celebrated through the fact that it felt like a mini festival within a pub at points. It was a space whose aim, and achievement, was to facilitate multiple interactions, moments of magic and feelings that could sometimes not be quantified. The role of social media, as Slam very correctly points out, creates a sense of false objectivity about what a story really represents. Whether it's the falsely portrayed glamour that veils the realities of people's lives, or the distorted sense of physical image many feel inclined to render to their followers, it makes complete sense why one wouldn't want a community with such a layered, deep and complex history "flattened" into "one linear narrative," through the lens of social media.

For a DIY community who ran events with a level of integrity that drove it, offering an egalitarian space to, now more well-known, acts such as King Krule, Yussef Dayes and Loyle Carner, whilst also providing a platform for artists who aren't as well-known, Slam's disenchantment with the "cherry-picking journalism that focuses on the London creative scene" led them to continuously "turn down journalists and be very idiosyncratic" in the way they chose to market an event that was community-based to the core. This liberated STEEZ from being assessed and defined, shifting the focus towards the subjective, and personal experience of the setting itself.

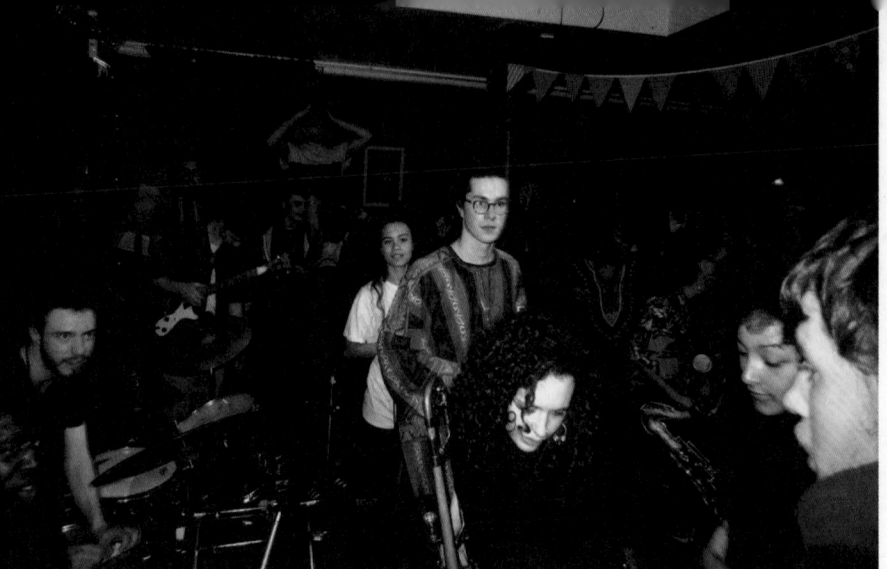

STEEZ – 28/2/16 – SE Dub Collective. From left to right: Femi Koleoso, Jake Long, Oscar Jerome, Poppy Ajudha, Jasmine Breinburg, Axel Kaner-Lidstrom, Rosie Turton, Nubya Garcia, Joe Armon-Jones. Hidden: Izzy Risk, Maxwell Owin, Jack Polley) at The Duke, Deptford. Photo credit: Beatrix Joyce

In a time where an Instagram story is the extent to which most people tell or receive their stories, or where accessing history has become over-accessible through devices which saturate us with information, there is a deeply profound virtue in the fact that an absolutely crucial part of London's recent cultural history can only be accessed through human voices and primitive storytelling. At a time where we, as humans, are failing to interact with each other in person, rather gaining information online, suddenly we are faced with a spectacle of recent history, in which the lack of a digital footprint forces us to learn this information from those who were present within the space. This in turn probes us to dig deeper to learn about it and allows the information we do receive to be more reliable and more personal, giving justice to a piece of the London puzzle whose richness isn't distilled into a reduced online framework. STEEZ's approach ensures that it is a sense of polyvocality that prevails over a univocality when understanding this story; something that harmonises with the scene's philosophy of allowing all voices to be heard in a representative way.

Whilst on the topic of social media, it is clear that the creative sector is one that is often painted with a false sense of perfection. The excitement of the line-ups being announced, the beauty of the event poster, the vibes from the videos. We, as the consumers of this culture, can easily become enamoured by the perfection that appears to envelop event runners and those behind the scenes. However, speaking to Lex in the months after TRC had lost its licence as a venue, it was clear that he had been faced with challenges that he wasn't comfortable opening up about, especially when wanting to portray the 'brand' as stable and held together with a sense of leadership. Lex mentions how he had recently conversed with Marina Blake about this, speaking about the importance of "differentiating yourself from the brand or the venue," referring to the stresses of upholding something that's public.

He tells me about a Facebook status he made after TRC lost its licence, writing that it was Hackney Council's decision to revoke it. Before he knew it, countless people were insulting the council on Twitter, articles were being written and he found himself "under a microscope" of intensity; the last thing he needed on one of the most stressful days he'd had.

"It's a human odyssey doing something like this," he tells me. "It's the human aspect which is most challenging... I think it's good for people to know about the difficult times." Whilst social media holds an unrealistic mirror up to communities, establishments and individuals, mental health issues and personal anxieties exist beneath such façades, growing at an exponential rate. Sharing a moment of reflection with Lex on some of the more unglamorous moments of what he does felt refreshing. Hopefully it can help start, and sustain, an important discussion about mental health in the arts. When our friends are posting about all of their achievements and exciting happenings, perhaps we should question what else may be occupying their life before presuming they are doing so well—a presumption that can often unhealthily propel our own anxiety, leading us to compare ourselves to those whose lives we see a fragment of, often in diluted form.

An engaged set of participants

Whilst the existence of social media has meant many live gigs and music events are met by an array of youth holding a blanket of mobile phones up to the performer these days, this community has thrived off maintaining a sense of engagement that has underpinned its experience and enhanced the quality of such moments. One reason I believe this is the case is due to the unconventional use of rules within some of these spaces. Rules that could be interpreted as assertive, yet have demanded a respect from all those present within the setting.

It becomes clear the effectiveness of rules when they are not just exercised by those who are running the night but by all those present within the setting. This can only happen when everybody feels a part of what is going on—something that is allowed through the lack of hierarchy in such spaces. When entering Steam Down on a Wednesday evening, huddling into a jam-packed setting, everybody is met by Wayne Francis speaking to all those present in the room prior to the music commencing. Following on from welcoming in all newcomers, he says the words, "If you want to talk..."

"GO OUTSIDE!" The crowd chant in response with intensity and belief. As a newcomer, you don't feel overpowered by a man at the front of the room telling you what to do. You recognise that it is a sentiment felt, and expressed, by all those around you. By not speaking, you are respecting the musicians as well as your fellow "participants", as Wayne refers to the crowd, in my conversation with him. Whilst many people treat environments such as live music venues as spaces of leisure where the music becomes a background presence—a casualised addition to the room that is aiding your chat with your mate—Wayne flips this preconception on its head by letting everybody know in a clear-cut way that if you want to be here, you simply must engage with what's going on in the room. And that starts with respecting all those around you by being quiet.

This corresponds to Errol Anderson's Touching Bass who published a manifesto for their club nights, outlining certain rules and notions that attendees were encouraged to familiarise themselves with. One of them was 'no phones on the dancefloor'. I ask him about this and wonder if previously working at Boiler Room, an entity centred around filming music and streaming it, caused him to have a sense of disenchantment and probed him to raise awareness about this. He tells me that was indeed the case and that the countless cameras would almost authorise those in attendance to do the same, which got suffocating at points.

"I'd look around the room and everyone would have their phones up. And I'd think, 'But you're here though?'... There is something to be said about just putting your phones away. And being with a group of people and just looking at each other and being like, 'this is sick' and just being present... Some of my favourite moments of life have just been when something has happened and then some time down the line, someone has been like, 'do you remember that moment...' There's no footage of it but it just happened and it's just as strong in your mind and memory. You can remember the smells. Why do you need to have a phone on the dancefloor?"

Errol makes a key point about the sensory aspect of memory. Sometimes having footage of a memory means we go straight to that to access the feelings we felt, or to tell the story. However, there is power in having to take your senses back to that moment, forcing us to access memory in the most personal way possible.

In my conversation with Wayne, I ask him about the significance of the 'no talking' rule at Steam Down and the need for all those present to obey it. "If you are here to listen to music and share space with other people that are also sharing or participating in the listening process... I feel it goes beyond just respecting the musicians. It goes on to respecting the environment and the whole space. If you all want to experience something from it, then you all have to be attentive to it. Because that is also a conversation that's happening to you, it's just not one with words. And you are meant to have a conversation back to it, but that conversation is not with chat, it's with your body, or it's with you singing, or a call and response."

Referring to the live music exchange as a 'conversation' is an acute metaphor. The reason 'the London jazz scene' has seen unprecedented levels of energy stem from it, is due to what organic live music allows; something that other, less fluid, artforms or musical styles may not afford. Jazz music is a flexible artform which is contingent on an exchange, and an engaged crowd enable this reciprocity to unfold, allowing the music be elevated to a place that couldn't be foreseen at the start of the gig. When the dancers shout, cut shapes, sweat and screw their faces, the musicians blow into their horns with a different intensity, they hit their drums with a different pulsation, they string their instruments and batter their keys; both parties are impacted by each other's spirit, creating an explosive energy which can't be quantified. A transfer of energy that is remarkably enhanced in settings where hierarchy isn't in existence. Steam Down doesn't involve a stage. Musicians and listeners stand facing each other in an intimate, arched space, thus, the transferal of energy is a lot easier to achieve and more magical when it does occur. Live music allows the musician and the listener to communicate in the most stripped-back, raw setting possible. A conversation as direct as it can be. Even more direct than listening to a record. And as major labels and commercial radios continue to lose the power that has seemed to monopolise the music industry for decades, the thirst for live music continues to grow.

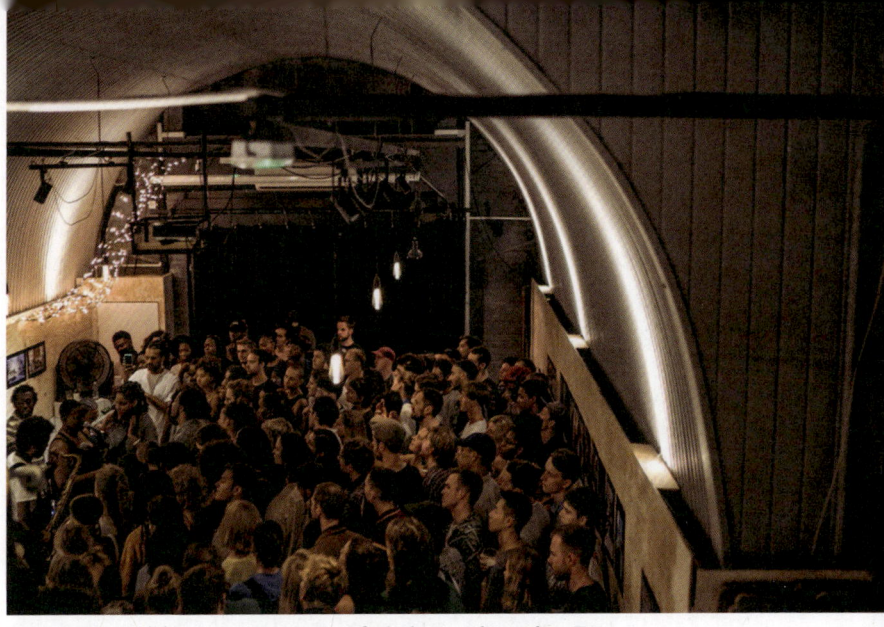

Steam Down – 22/8/18 – Buster Mantis, Deptford. Photo credit: Andrew Testa

The exchange that jazz affords; the force of the physical setting

This idea of the 'exchange' is something I believe is harder to achieve in something like electronic music. And that is why this scene has been consumed by the attention, curiosity and excitement that it has. At a time where every song in the world is at our fingertips and we aren't faced with the requirement of having to go into a record shop to buy our music, as previous generations were made to do, we consume such art through intangible mediums which over-saturate us and lead us to not appreciate the depth of what we're hearing. Whilst recent research has shown that one in four songs played on Spotify is skipped within the first five seconds, a fact that shines a light on our dwindling attention spans, a rule as clear-cut as Wayne's 'no talking on the dancefloor' or Errol's 'no phones on the dancefloor' evidently has its unequivocal value. Attendees of such culture are finding it fascinating to see music, literally, created in front of them, at a time where the over-accessibility of technology seems to be supplying us with innumerable DJs and producers.

There is a human fulfilment and satisfaction in knowing that the saxophonist in front of you has had to practice for four hours a day for the last few years in order to do what they are doing that evening. People are becoming compelled and lifted by this fact due to its authentic human element. This is also why this scene has forged such a strong identity, due to the time it has taken the musicians to get to where they are—a fact indicative of the timelessness of the music's sound.

Following a 15-year period of technology's boom, suddenly there is a movement back towards the physical and this London live music scene has happened to embody this sense of physicality that people are desiring. Something that is highlighted by the increase of vinyl sales: 4.3 million sales in the UK in 2019, marking the 12th consecutive year of growth, whilst the USA has seen a 2000% increase in vinyl sales in the period of 2006 to 2019.

Despite the movement back towards the physical product and the desire for the live setting growing, it is clear that this scene is recognised and appreciated by a minority of people in the bigger picture. I recall an anecdote to Lex in Episode 3 about an Uber Pool journey I took a couple of years ago alongside two strangers. I mention how this girl asked me what I had been up to that evening, and I responded by telling her I was at a gig. Her response was, "You went to a gig? What is the point of going all the way out to see music when you can just sit at home and listen to music on your laptop?" I was befuddled and simply couldn't find the words to respond as she left the cab—a departure which was gratefully welcomed by both me and the cab driver. I recall it to Lex and we laugh about it. However, I raise the fascinating and important fact that it illustrates certain people may think in such a way and although that may seem a world away from us, it's something we must crucially acknowledge since the convenience of technology is making this feeling more commonplace than we'd like to think.

I ask Lex something simple. "What is the beauty of people coming together for something like live music?" He compares the idea of being "on your own" to "connecting with someone," the latter of which he explains is "the most powerful thing you can do to feel good. Even if you are depressed. And it's not an easy thing to do," he continues. "You have to push yourself." But that feeling is simply unparalleled and it's an attitude which is encapsulated by esteemed actor Mark Rylance in a recent interview he did with The Times.

Speaking about why he wouldn't be as sad if cinemas all close, compared to theatres, following the impact of the Coronavirus outbreak, Rylance says, "When I go out, I want to go to something live. I want to have the soul of the person in the room. And though there is soul in film, it isn't in the room with you. At a great play, opera or piece of live music there is a collective consciousness, in my experience, that's in the room. It's different than cinema," he concludes. This idea of the soul being "in the room" is exactly what creates, what Rylance refers to as, the "collective consciousness". A unity that is to an extent limited when a screen is involved; acting as a barrier that prevents a two-way exchange. And after a period of time where all of the entertainment we have consumed has been via the medium of the screen, I believe a mass shift towards the physical is incoming. Hopefully such spaces will be protected, and still exist post-Corona, in order to facilitate this.

A template to increase engagement

What this London creative sphere has shown is that a collective consciousness combined with increased levels of engagement can be the key ingredients for creating something unique and personal. Errol Anderson's Touching Bass hosted a series of events they called 'Speaking in Sound' at the wonderful Brilliant Corners in Dalston, east London. It was a residency that aimed to slow down the pace with which we consume music. It occurred on a Monday evening and would combine discussions, that explored topics such as 'the neuroscience of improvisation', alongside intimate musical performances and annotated DJ sets, whereby selectors would shed light on the context of the music they were playing whilst those present would lie back on beanbags and get lost in the music's frequencies. It was also strictly alcohol-free.

I was fascinated by the removal of something as seemingly inextricable from one's experience of music as alcohol and asked Errol about this. "There is an unhealthy relationship between our experience in a club space and drinking. There needs to be a reconfiguration of why you are entering a club space," he tells me. Being offered the space to do such an event highlights the forward-thinking nature of an establishment as progressive as Brilliant Corners. Earlier in the conversation, when speaking about the nature of most of their crowd not being big drinkers, Errol told me that the statement the Touching Bass crew would often hear from venues was, "we really like your crowd but we are just not making enough money on the bar," creating a frustrating conflict of interests within the crew, wanting to focus on the

Tounching Bass 'Speaking in Sound' – 15/5/17 – featuring Yussef Dayes, Nubya Garcia, Wayne Francis, Shirley Tetteh, Dave Koor at Brilliant Corners, Dalston. Photo credit: Alex Rita

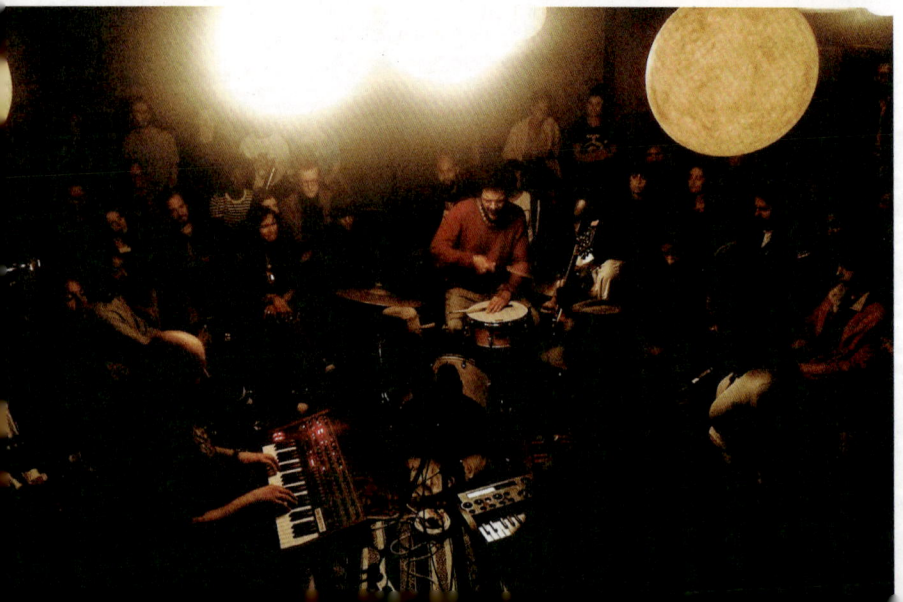

music whilst also wanting the venue to be happy too, to ensure they would be invited back. However, 'Speaking in Sound' allowed Touching Bass to help "re-root the understanding" of why and how we should consume music, taking it back to the source—the sound.

There is a clear correlation between unsocial hours of the week offering culture and the increased engagement with which it is met by those present. There's something powerful about Speaking in Sound being an event that occurred on a Monday evening. Or Steam Down happening at 8pm on a Wednesday. Or STEEZ being at 7pm on a Sunday. Suddenly the role of a component such as alcohol is less influential in the evening's proceedings and there's an inevitable shift in focus towards the culture that's being offered, heightening people's connection to it. I had a chat with Gilles Peterson recently about his seminal club night 'That's How It Is,' which he co-ran with James Lavelle weekly from 1993-2006 as a Monday night residency at Bar Rumba on Shaftesbury Avenue in Soho. It was clear to me the significance of it being on a Monday. Its less social time in the week attracted a more committed crowd who came with better intentions, "focused more towards the music", Gilles told me. It appears that such events have a heightened level of engagement not necessarily because they separate the wheat from the chaff, so to say, but because they allow the chaff to access their inner wheat, if you know what I mean. Something that I think is beautifully profound.

Rewriting the rulebook; shedding barriers

Conversing with both fashion designer Nicholas Daley and musician, DJ and radio broadcaster (and my sister) Nabihah Iqbal in Episode 1 of Mare Street Records, we spoke about how Nicholas has helped redefine what the experience of a fashion show is. Showcasing his Autumn/Winter 2018 collection 'Red Clay' at a Swiss church in Covent Garden on a Monday afternoon, for London Fashion Week, he assembled a group of musicians together. Shabaka Hutchings, Yussef Dayes, Mansur Brown, Alfa Mist and James Massiah rocked the threaded garments as they engaged in four improvised jam sessions over the period of an afternoon. The clothing collection made a link between the London jazz renaissance of now, and the relationship between the 70s soul-jazz musicians and the clothes worn by them, whilst the collection's title is a nod at Freddie Hubbard's prolific 1970 album.

It wasn't a showcase dominated by a catwalk which had the most elite guests in the front row. It was a coming together of the world's fashion press and Nicholas's friends, their friends and his family, as all elitist barriers that dominate the idea of a fashion show were torn down, subverting the preconceptions many of us had of what such an experience was meant to entail. Nicholas tells me that his favourite moment of the afternoon was when drummer Yussef Dayes stood up and exclaimed that "this does not feel like a fashion show." For Nicholas this was the "seal of approval" that confirmed he had achieved what he had set out to do, bringing his clothes to life through a multi-sensory experience that made you captivatingly watch the musicians' movement and clothes, listen to the rhythms of the instruments' sound, and smell the burning incense in the room. Every fashion show he's curated since has harboured the same template, having influenced various other designers in the process.

This fearless approach of rewriting the rulebook, straying away from the expectations of convention, is exactly what has made this scene so groundbreaking. Whilst Nicholas has done this in fashion, Marina Blake starting a festival at the age of 19 and maintaining it as an intimate entity which serves a grassroots purpose has helped redefine, to many, what a festival represents. As a structure that is associated with often overpowering the attendee with its size and separation, Brainchild has acted as a means of light to many, aligning live music, DJs, theatre, poetry and political conversation in an environment as

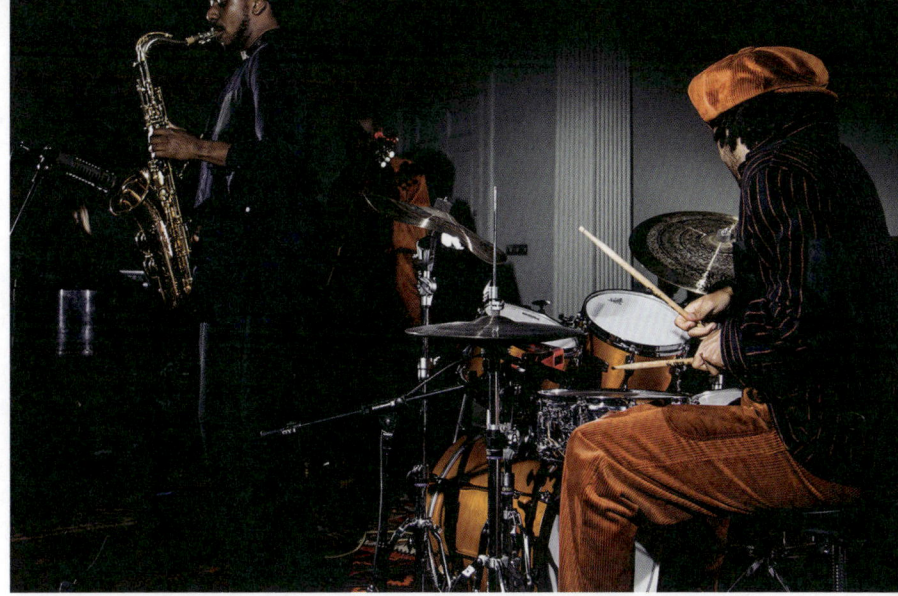

Nicholas Daley 'Red Clay' fashion show – 8/1/18 – Shabaka Hutchings, Mansur Brown and Yussef Dayes at The Swiss Church, Covent Garden. Photo credit: Ben Awin/HYPEBEAST

unpressured as one's back garden. She has offered a platform for a pioneering music scene, that is now internationally recognised, to find its voice. And has also offered a safe space to many, such as myself, to feel like your voice can be used, heard and valued.

Steam Down has flipped the common presumption of a jazz night, as a passive chin-stroking experience, into something propelled by the energy associated with a grime night. As mosh-pits and crowd-surfing have been frequent, natural products of the levels of energy reached at certain points, the organic influence of London's musical melting pot, such as grime, afrobeat and dub elements, has fuelled a weekly meditation unparalleled to many. By breaking down barriers historically associated with the word 'jazz', Wayne has helped masses of people feel part of something special, relaxed and not snobby. This idea has been seen across the entities I have explored, from STEEZ to Touching Bass and Total Refreshment Centre too—these spaces are irrefutable in their complete significance of serving society as a positive force.

The forward-thinking figures I've been privileged to speak to, who have helped spearhead this movement without realising it at the time, have shifted the way many have been able to perform art and consume it. Through eliminating hierarchy and taking risks, the blossoming of an initial seed into an embellished tree has been due to the fact that it is the people who have been at the centre of this movement. People from all kinds of places. Who have been constantly welcomed in. And continue to be valued. They have all recognised the power of joining together and tuning into something greater than themselves.

And whilst this country remains divided on many issues and large groups of us feel disillusioned with the "defunct" nature of political leadership, as Marina Blake puts it, we can find hope and light in communities being able to come together through the medium of the arts, irrespective of background, race, class, gender or sexual orientation. Through spaces that allow us to connect to ourselves and those around us in an honest way. Spaces in which historically elite barriers are being torn down; where spectators and performers aren't separated physically or figuratively. Where conversations can be had, stories can

Touching Bass x Eglo Records party – 7/9/19 – Simulacra Studio, Brixton.
Photo credit: Errol Anderson

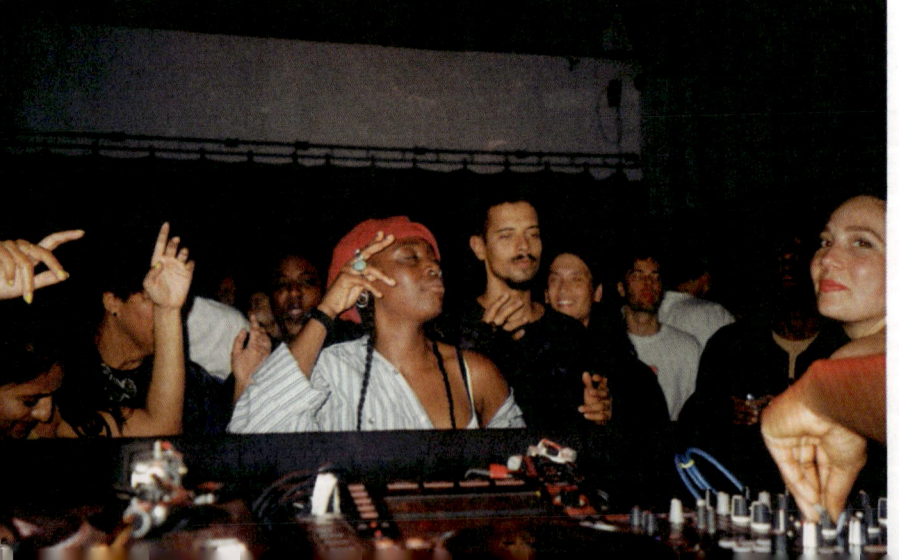

be told and opinions can be voiced; all through the means of an exchange. These are the spaces that truly form the backbone of our country's fabric, so let's take care of them.